CLARITY OF
GOALS
AND VISION

Unfolding Clarity in Your Life and Business

SANTIMA JASPER

CGV PUBLISHING HOUSE

CGV Publishing House LLC
Leesburg, Florida, 34748

ISBN: 979-8-9876369-0-9 (Paperback)
ISBN: 979-8-9876369-1-6 (Ebook)

Printed in the United States Of America

CONTENTS

INTRODUCTION

Living in Clarity is the world I saw in my vision. But I didn't know how to get there. My life and business felt overwhelming and unclear. I struggled with limiting beliefs, doubts, and obstacles. *How did I get here and why? Where do I want to be? Where do I deserve to be? Where do I desire to be? How do I get to the life in my vision?* These are the questions I started to ask myself. I desired to have more–to have what I want, deserve, and dream about. I embarked on a journey to Clarity with determination and passion. I now share what I learned on my journey to Clarity with you. This book is for you and about you and *your unique success.* Thank you for the privilege of joining you on your journey to Clarity.

CHAPTER 1

My Story

The Beginning of My Entrepreneurial Journey

"What kind of space can I turn this into?" I asked myself as I looked at my backyard. My husband helped me see the vision of what my backyard could look like. I was intrigued. That's what I want for you, as you read this book and do the exercises, I want you to visualize the finished product before you have it.

A couple weeks later he finished the landscaping work he had promised me. I had never seen anything so nicely put together in a backyard. He turned it into a beautiful garden. Beautiful landscape around the 3 big magnolia trees that bloom white flowers during the late spring and summer season. Bougainvillea's crawling up on a white trellis that bloom magenta pink and annuals that bloom in its season with columns and white marble rock with ground cover plants that made our backyard transform into an oasis garden. A beautiful backyard that looks like it could be put in a home and garden magazine. He owned a landscape business, and I was curious about his work and wanted to learn more. I would tag along and watch as my vision began to expand.

In contrast, I had an office job at a bank. Getting fired from my bank teller position after three years and after finding out I was pregnant for the third time wasn't the ideal way I thought my dream job would end. I had mixed feelings at first. I needed this break away from what I had been doing for the past three years. Plus, they weren't big on ranking up. I was ready to try something new and experience progression in the banking industry, but it wasn't happening. I was ok with it, but after I had my son, it was time to get back to work.

I did some long thinking about going back into the corporate world and banking was the only thing I could think of, so I put in applications to almost every bank in my city. I was declined by every bank. That left me with an empty feeling like I wasn't good enough and no one wanted to hire me. I didn't want a regular job. I wanted a job that I could turn into a career. It didn't quite work out that way. So, I thought about helping my other half with his business.

He had been talking about how "the guys just don't see what he sees" and "they're just there for a check" and I knew this business meant everything to him. So, I asked him the question, but I was very hesitant thinking how hard it could be to hear the word *no* if he said it. Not only did he say *no*, but he laughed and said that would never work! I don't take no very well as an answer anyhow, so I showed him what I could do rather than getting any further into why he didn't think it would work.

Male-Dominated Field

I was starting from zero. I knew nothing about what I was getting myself into, but I took my job very seriously and learned everything in the landscaping business inside and out. I visualized myself doing the job, knowing the tools, and becoming the best and hardest worker my partner has ever had. And over time that's exactly what happened. I went even further than just knowing the fundamentals. I did things he didn't ask of me that helped the business grow beyond what we could see in the moment. I also applied the education I had from business degree courses. I was taking these courses to get into a higher position in the banking industry is what I thought. Now looking back this was only preparing me for the business and businesses I would one day own. I earned the right to own my own business.

I worked hard, but there were times I felt shut out in a male-dominated industry. But I kept my head high. The guys we hired would be amazed by how hard I worked but didn't want to follow my lead. They didn't accept me. Well, I couldn't care less. It was my business. But I would be lying if I said I didn't truly care because I wanted to build a solid team and I wanted to know what I was doing wrong. Over the years I would find out that it wasn't me. It was them. This wasn't their business, so they didn't have ten toes down in the business like I did. This was how I took care of my family, and this was my *life*.

I would go into home improvement stores and get the look of rejection and men would act like I didn't exist. They weren't so welcoming, and I didn't know why. I once was asked, "Hey Santima do you think you should be doing this? How do you think people are really looking at you?" Now that question, I truly didn't care for. I was too deep into what I had learned during eight years, diving deep into what continued to feel like a passion. But my cup started to get emptied.

But before we get into that, I saw pivotal moments we needed to make in the business going from lawn and landscape services to a full handyman home improvement service. We had the skills and our customers demanded it and over time we transitioned, and it was the best pivot we ever made. Our team didn't like the shift which lead to them eventually firing themselves.

Her 24/7 Partner

Being in business with my husband and business partner has been a life learning journey and it's been very adventurous. We have come to know each other inside and out and learned that we don't like to be apart for too long. Of course, it has its hard times, but the good times outweigh the hard times by far. We learned each other's strengths and weaknesses and complimented each other's strong points. We became an inseparable power couple that love what we do together. Keeping up with life and business became a challenge with the need to balance it all. But how? I became very curious and embarked on a journey I was always passionate about.

Trying New Things

I became so great with what I was doing in the landscape business that I wanted to discover my own passions. I was great at a lot of things. I started doing hair. Then I did make-up for proms, birthdays, and graduations. That lead to me to opening an online store selling products I enjoyed using. Later I worked at a makeup store because I wanted to learn how to build a beauty business, so that I could one day run my own. Then I realized I just wanted to choose one thing that was meaningful and that would be the change I wanted to see in the world.

I started listening to audios and reading tons of books on self and professional development. I had no idea this was out there. The very first motivational audio I heard was from Eric Thomas. He sparked a different energy I've never heard before, my kind of energy and before I knew it, I was listening to all his motivational audios and learned so much that I didn't want to stop learning.

The pandemic hit and it was time to take life seriously. Before the pandemic, my online beauty store was getting lots of traffic but when the pandemic transpired my store took a hit which forced me to put my store on hold. That's when I decided to get into life insurance. Life insurance changed my life because of the income it gave me, but it wasn't what I was passionate about. I sold more than a few policies before I told myself I wouldn't give my time and energy away to something that wasn't 100% my vision and dreams. There's a saying that if you can sell life insurance you can sell *anything*. I stopped selling life insurance and started searching for the thing I was most passionate about deep down inside. *But what was it?*

Finding My Own Passion

Not everyone knows exactly what their passionate about at first. I sure enough didn't know exactly, but I knew I was good at lots of things because I put my mind and energy into it and gave it my all. I knew I worked hard, but it was time to turn hard work into work I enjoyed without the physical labor. So, I started digging deeper within myself. My mentors through books and audios I've read over time helped me find the patience to understand that it would take me time to find my passion and clarity. But it would be the thing that had always been a passion of mine. It had been swept up underneath the rug for so long because I would listen to what others thought I should be and do for a long time. Until I realized that I needed to direct myself towards where I desired to be along with faith.

So, I reflected on my past and wrote it down on paper and it turned into me journaling. With journaling, I started to understand myself in ways I've never understood before. As I continued to write and have a book filled with my thoughts and reflecting on my past and now, I realized something I wanted and was passionate about. Not because everyone else told me that I would do good if I did this or that, but because it was something that I said I wanted to do. It felt amazing to reach back in time to that little girl who said she wanted to be a teacher. I would play school with my siblings until they became tired of me. They became so tired of me that they knew not to ask me what game I wanted to play ever again.

Childhood Dream

Do you remember the time your teacher, family and friends asked you what you wanted to be when you grew up? And do you remember what it was that you told them? For me it was a teacher for the longest time, until I noticed that I didn't get the same reaction some of the other kids got when they said they wanted to be a doctor or a lawyer. As children we are designed to be people pleasers and say the right things to get noticed or be acknowledged. So, when someone asked me, I tried not to answer. I tried not to even speak. I didn't like the idea of being looked at as if I was better or less than others. I kept those thoughts to myself and said *I don't know*. I notice many kids say what they think grown-ups may want to hear today.

I encourage my own children to say what they want to be and to believe in themselves whole heartedly. But know it takes hard work dedication and focus to be and do what your heart desires and make sure you give it your all. I found my passion going back into my childhood and reflecting on the thing that made me most happy. It took some time to realize it, but I was determined. Now I needed to find clarity, but I wouldn't know it until I continued to journal my life and write what I was thinking and feeling and take more than a few trips down memory lane. Not only did I look at my past, but I also wrote it out and I did this many times until I started to see patterns I'd never seen before.

Finding Clarity

I was determined to seek clarity in my life and my business but I didn't know how to. It always felt as though something was missing and I was going to find clarity no matter how long it took me. I started digging deeper into myself and managing my time because I started to enjoy being with myself. I couldn't believe that I didn't know what that was like! I started loving me for the person I am and the person that I am becoming. As I continued to read more books and listen to more audios, I started to take action developing a positive growth mindset, becoming an optimistic thinker, as I became the leader I needed to be for myself in order to evolve. We must continue to learn, but not only learn, to listen along the journey and the path that has been cut out for you. I kept hearing and seeing the word *goals* and I had never intentionally set a goal on paper to plan it or write it out. I had just started doing the thing I wanted to do.

I came across a book called "Goals and Vision Mastery." This book is filled with some of our top leaders here with us today and a lifetime before our time. It gave me Clarity! My mind opened in so many ways that were closed off. These ideas were there inside me all along they were just closed off and this book opened many doors for me. It helped me discover my passion, my purpose, and how to get to my desired goal. Today I've read the mastery book six times and I'm excited to read it again. I decided to name my business *Clarity of Goals and Vision* and to take this name as something that was given to me in a precious way a gift given to me by leaders of this world that gave back in a tremendously impactful way. Nothing happens automatically. You must be willing to put in the work and manage it.

My mind started to become extremely creative, and I of course continued to learn and I'm a researcher at heart. I believe if I want to know something I need to seek the information, learn about it and research it. Not that no one has ever told me but because it's my responsibility to seek what I desire to know now. We are not taught all the lessons we need to learn as we discover the unknown and demand answers right away along our journey. The answer lies within your unique journey as the lessons unfold. No matter how old you are it's never too late to unfold clarity as you continue along the path that was designed for you! As my thoughts became clear and even more creative, the more I learned, was the more I developed the urge to start teaching others. I developed the urge to start teaching what was working for me so that others could do it to. Again, I reflected on the things that helped me get where I am today and saw that there was so much clarity in what I was doing. I developed a system that gets you from where you are now to where you desire to be. I created the acronym CLARITY to help you reach your goals.

- Clear
- Logic
- Action
- Reflect/ Revisit/ Revise
- Improving
- Transforming
- Yourself

The Clarity method helped me to see a clear path and journey. It helped me understand my goals and my vision on a deeper level of my unique success in what I define my philosophy and declare success to be for myself. It can help you too is the reason for me writing this book. While writing this book I wanted to put you up to the challenge with the 7 Day Clarity Challenge. In this challenge you'll discover a small transformation that will guide you into one of your biggest goals. I help you organize your visualization, prepare, create your unique Masterplan, and set the goal to action. Ready to take action? Type in your web browser https://clarityofgoalsandvision/7daychallenge.com. See you there! I wrote this book because I had the uncontrollable urge to share my story with you to help you get the things you want in your life and in your business.

In addition to the CLARITY Method, I developed the GPS Method and the Clarity Cause and Effect method. I designed all of these to work together to help you cast the vision for your goals and create the reality you desire. I share all of this with you in the next upcoming chapters.

The Uncontrollable Urge

I had the uncontrollable urge to start my next business that would help inspire many women to pursue their vision and goals through clarity and taking you from where you are now to where you desire to be.

Sometimes we get stuck. Because we don't know which direction we are going. We look to people in our lives because we feel that they know us the best. I had the uncontrollable urge to get unstuck to find clarity and share my journey with you. Now that we are finally here, I also had the uncontrollable urge to write this book the beginning of this year, but God had a different plan. But he saw to it that this book got written this year. I say this to ask you, "What is your foundation built on and how will you determine and manage what's for you now and what's for you in your future?" In this book we will go deeper into your now and your future.

Helping Struggling Families

In my vision I saw myself helping struggling families. My family struggled and I grew up wanting to know more and do better for myself and my family. Until I saw this opportunity in a much bigger way. It wasn't just my family in a struggle there are many families in a struggle, and I would like to help as many families as I can along my journey. It rested in my heart so well and I started to visualize building communities and programs. This is what I desire and is the reason behind what I enjoy doing today. My goal is to help my first hundred families and get people to join me on this journey. As many people this message comes by, I can impact in a much bigger way is the bigger vision. I can be the change I want to see in the world!

CHAPTER 2

Your Journey to Clarity

"Trust your instincts. Intuition doesn't lie."

- OPRAH WINFREY

Clarity for Life and Business

We work towards clarity, not work against it. Let me tell you a little more of what I mean by this. We can get overwhelmed. Things start getting unclear over time not in one day. Your whole life can pass you by and you didn't realize just how confusing things are and why you never managed to get the things you truly desire. For all my entrepreneurs, business can get a bit foggy making it difficult to keep track of your life. After all, your business maintains your life, gives you the many options you look forward to through having financial freedom.

But through the years of managing, some things get out of our control. Whether the contributing factors be because of life or business. I like to say that without having clarity in your personal life it's hard to maintain clarity in your business and the same goes the other way around.

In order to have a balance between the two, we have to understand the relationship between them both and respect boundaries that can get intertwined, at times causing another layer of confusion. I believe that managing a business can be overwhelming even if you love and have a passion for what you do. It's the passion that keeps you going through the hard work. And I believe you must understand your life and the boundaries you set in place. When you're at work you're focused on work and when you're on vacation you're on vacation. Maintaining both parts of your life and being aware of where you are with both business and personal life is extremely important. They can distract from each other or work together. Clarity, Focus, and Alignment is my method to getting back on track from a distracted world when all the odds seem to be against you.

How Leaders Find Clarity

Leaders like Oprah focus on being the change they want to see in the world. Their focus sets an example of how and what moving closer to clarity in your life and business looks like.

Other industry leaders like Amy Porterfield, our lovely humble and true to her authentic self, America's vegan mom Tabitha Brown, Jenna Kutcher, Ree Drummond (The Pioneer Woman), each of these give us examples of women entrepreneurs with worldwide influence who took a chance and started their own businesses.

Where to Start?

They say "just start" but sometimes we don't always know where to start. Whether it's a new business, maintaining your business, setting new goals, or taking action etc. I believe everyone's journey is unique to their own path. To just start, you must be willing to learn and want to know some new things. You must have a deeper desire to want to become even more than what you see on the surface. I believe that saying "just start" can cripple some people while others soar, which can bring you to questioning yourself. Those questions will lead to doubt, confusion, fear, negativity, hurt, pain, anxiety, depression, uncertainty, and unwanted pressures.

For me, when I did find my passion, it wasn't about just starting, it was more so about being impactful from the start and to be authentic to myself and the people I'm leading. But how do I drown out the loud noise that becomes overwhelming and sets me 10ft back? *Intention.* What are your intentions and what is the goal that you're working towards right now? Now get focused on the goal with a narrow, fine-tuned focus. Every day becomes a new day, and you learn something new about the progress of your goal each day. That's the transformation coming to life right before your eyes and it's the opportunity you get to appreciate in the moment every day.

Looking at other people getting to their desired destination won't quite get us there as it will motivate us all for a couple of minutes and then fade away as fast as our mind moves forward to the next thing that needs to get done throughout our day. So, each day you start on your goal you get to learn about yourself, your values, and the goal. Each day you are becoming and improving your desired outcome. "Just starting" for you may look like just starting on your goal. But there is a preparation process that needs to go on behind the scenes. By understanding where you are now and what that end goal really looks like. Then there is the part where you get to visualize what your preparation steps look like. Finally, you get to feel yourself being and doing in that moment. By doing all of this you make your goal ten times more likely to become your reality. You have prepared yourself for your start and now you are not just starting. You are *prepared* to start.

In my younger days I've said it. *I'm going to be rich, but I didn't know how.* I'm going to have a very good paying job but didn't know what that job was going to be. I'm going to be a model just because everyone said I looked like one but never new how. There was no vision for the steps I would take to get there and nothing in sight that would prepare me for the just starting phase while I was told to just start my whole adult hood life with absolutely no direction. I believe there is a starting from scratch phase and a phase where you are an expert in your field, but you feel that you want to be more prepared for the next steps giving you space to open yourself up for other opportunities to take place is how I saw it.

The idea of understanding that I can be prepared and open myself for many other opportunities to take place was the secret gold mine for me. I didn't want to go the traditional path everyone else was trailblazing towards my desires and success. Especially since the crowd was saying one thing but my leaders were showing and telling me another. So, as you continue to embark on your desired journey, you can do it with clarity, focus, and alignment and we'll get more into these three methods that create your world of endless opportunities.

Is Taking the Leap Encouraging or Discouraging?

Taking the leap can be both encouraging and discouraging, leaving you with an array of mixed emotions about the process and never starting on your ideas, your dreams, your vision, your goals. It's like being in the sea with no one around to save you and fearing the worst will happen to you. Taking the leap is like just starting only you're taking that action and your taking massive action in taking the leap. Only just like starting, taking the leap can feel like imposter syndrome. Taking the leap, taking action but not feeling like you know enough to do what you love to do, and the rewards can sometimes make you feel undeserving. That's were having clarity comes in and helps you realize, understand, and focus on where you are now and where you desire to be. You feel like you are not enough, or an imposter are just illusions and unwanted circumstances that aren't apart of our journey. We shouldn't let them slow us down from getting closer to our accomplishments and achievements.

Principles top leaders use for clarity and finding your own journey

Clarity is the first thing we begin with when we start anything. It has helped top leaders with charting their course, while mapping out their destination, and achieving great levels of success upon their wildest dreams. I compiled seven principles together as I did some long research and strategically put this framework together that would allow us to follow step by step. This is the CLARITY acronym mentioned in Chapter 1. It's what this book is all about.

- **C**larity
- **L**ogic
- **A**ction
- **R**eflect/ Revisit/ Revise
- **I**mproving
- **T**ransforming
- **Y**ourself

Of course, it will take time to build a relationship with the clarity method and build it into your everyday life practice.

"One of the best ways to build a new habit is to identify a current habit you already do each day and then stack your new behavior on top. This is called habit stacking."

- JAMES CLEAR

My hope is that this book will be a gift, a book to read multiple times, maybe even to give to a friend that is ready to go from career to starting her business she is passionate about. Or a stay-at-home mom that likes the idea of starting a business but needs clarity and direction. The need for clarity is within us all.

Is Clarity Perfection?

Clarity does not aim for perfection it aims to unfold. There was a time where I thought clarity was perfection. Further into seeking information, my own experiences, and more research over the years led me to sum it all up with one word, unfold. Each day I had an intentional zoomed in focus on the Masterplan not to seek perfection but to seek clarity that unfolded daily. This guided me into a world filled with an abundance of opportunities I wouldn't have seen before. I also felt as though when seeking help on my journey it was more of me seeking approval. My brand strategist helped me understand that I was affirming not seeking approval. And in that she was exactly right. And after she said that things started to align. It wasn't perfection, it was *preparation*. It wasn't approval it was *affirming*. We make up all these illusions in our minds and become over-critical within ourselves which limits us from getting what we desire to have and the outcome we set for ourselves. We put the final touches of limitations on ourselves and define it as perfection which slows down the goal process that eventually puts a hold on what we desire and the Masterplan that was created.

I hear so many people saying they're perfectionists, when really, they are *dream snatchers*. We put limits on ourselves, so we don't endure the pain we are afraid to feel. Procrastination is the result. We try to fix things because of the anxiety we create around being a perfectionist. Then we have a negative mindset on just about everything. Clarity is about having consistency in a positive state of mind and state of being.

How Clarity Helps you with Preparation

When preparing for the thing you desire, it gives you the clarity and the direction you thought you never had. With clarity, you're able to navigate your unique journey through a clear GPS that guides you. Even if you get off track, you have this GPS navigation that helps you go back to clarity and helps you reflect, revisit, and revise your next steps. As you prepare, you want to reflect and revise as you go because you continue to learn new things along your journey. This reflection creates a path that helps you take a deeper look into the map you created so that you can zoom in on the next left or right turn you will make. This makes decision-making so much easier and my favorite word of all- *effortless.* In order to get here, you have to be in a true relationship with both yourself *and* with clarity.

Your Dreams Lead You to Your Clearest Path

We have dreams that turn into ideas that turn into our most passionate vision but how do we turn it into our clear path? The first step is to turn that vision into goals and create the steps needed to get to our desired goal. But the steps to our clearest path doesn't just end there. We'll get in depth with the steps to your clearest path in later chapters with one of them being Reflection. Looking back to reflect on your improvements and making necessary revisions for what doesn't work to move forward in a clear direction and a clear path is important. The top leaders have several different achievable paths they can take whether they're taking a risk or their pivoting along their journey. Taking action, of course, is going to gain you some traction all while reflecting each week or even every day. It is going to help you understand your clearest path altogether. This also creates alignment that is often missed in the beginning of the start-up journey of a business if you decide to start one or if you already have started..

CHAPTER 3

Casting the Vision

From Dream to Idea

Do you believe that your dreams can come true? Well In this chapter, I want to give you the confidence to know you can dream big and your dreams can come true. You can turn your dreams into your vision of the future. Your dreams can come from a stimulating thought. It's the core center of who you truly are and gives you a sense of meaning and purpose that you desire to pursue. Unlocking your dream potential that's within you can feel discomforting at times when you're facing fear of failure or even fear of success. The best way to overcome a fear is believing in yourself and having a clear vision that gives you purpose and fulfillment. Dreams are closely associated with success and this book helps you get close and personal with *your* unique success.

All great things take time. It took time for you to be where you are right now. There was a process, different stages from beginning to end on how you were made to be born to bring you into this world. To a world that is filled with opportunities made just for you. Another example is baking a cake. You have instructions to prepare in the process of baking a cake. You can also decide which pan style you would like to bake your cake. Each type of cake has preparation steps for that specific process. You start with the ingredients you need to use in order to make a delicious, moist cake.

This process is also narrowed to the specific cake of your liking: chocolate, vanilla, red velvet, upside down pineapple cake, angel cake etc. So yes, even cake has preparation instructions down to the very point of eating the cake. If the cake isn't baked and the ingredients aren't mixed perfectly in their right order down to putting the cake in the oven you will not have a mouthwatering moist cake that rocks your world and gives you what your heart desires up until the very moment you been craving for your favorite cake. And yes, it also takes time to bake a cake. You patiently wait all of every minute and second it says to bake.

So now back to life and business. We are too impatient when it comes to mixing our own ingredients in our lives and businesses to ever see it come to how we truly pictured and dreamed of it to be. Throughout this entire book are the simple ingredients to bring your dreams into your unique reality. The cool thing about it is you don't have to start from scratch you can start from right where you are now.

"As long as your dreams appeal more to you than your fears, you will find the energy and courage to move on."

-INEKE VAN LINT

From idea to your vision. The ancients understood these principles. "Where there is no vision the people perish."

-PROVERBS 29:18

Where Your Vision Can Take You

Your vision can take you to your desired destination if you let it. The secret to turning your vision into your true reality is to open the floodgates to new opportunity. There are frameworks, guides and systems in this book that help you prepare, and preparation is key to success when you want to go far.

Your Vision Can Become Your Reality

The first step is to have the right positive growth mindset. Carol Dweck talks about growth mindset. She contrasts a fixed mindset with a growth mindset. When you have a vision, it is vital to connect the dots and take action. Having a mentor or a guide for this process helps speed and automate the process, of course. As your vision becomes your reality picture it like the house or the beautiful apartment you live in. Someone had the vision and the blueprint for it and brought that vision into reality. They hired all the right specialists that could also see that vision. Bringing people together that see the same vision you see multiplies the results you will receive. The reaping benefits and rewards become great royalties that sometimes come in many unexpected ways and that's the beauty in great things that happen for you.

> *"The passion for stretching yourself and sticking to it, even (or especially) when it's not going well, is the hallmark of the growth mindset."*
>
> -CAROL DWECK

Vision-Goals-Vision

Your vision starts at a surface level until it gets drawn out into the goal that spells out your steps and objectives.

Going right back into the vision, along your journey, you take action with your objectives and steps. This helps you hold your vision in place all while exercising and strengthening your vision. Here's where new opportunities become visual as you strengthen your will to take action to see a much more structured vision along your journey. So, it looks like this model:

- Surface Vision
- Goal
- Objective
- Steps
- Vision becomes more structured
- Repeat

Just as well, you have to exercise your body in order to keep your bones strong and keep your body young and healthy. It's the same concept for your vision with managing and keeping that vision strong and healthy.

Reflecting Your Vision Towards Your Desired Destination

Your vision turns into your roadmap towards your destination and the process of getting there. It supports the purpose and direction of your life and business-just as we connect our phones to our GPS app to get to our desired destination. As we type in the street name or if you're taking a road trip typing in the city and state will give you a roadmap to navigate you through streets, highways, and through cities places you've never been. You trust this GPS system to take you to your desired destination. And I will tell you and be perfectly honest with you, I always arrived at my destination seamlessly 99.9% of the time. Sometimes I ended up across the street somewhere and circled around 4 or 5 times before I actually found my destination. But I can say I've arrived at my desired destination and never got stranded or lost.

Using this same concept while turning our vision into a roadmap that gets us to our desired destination 99.9% of the time safely and the rest is a risk. In life and business there is always a risk we take. It's the prepared risks we take that bring our most wildly successful journeys to realization. .

Your Vision Becomes Your Goal

As you turn your vision into your goals, you then turn them into achievable steps and objectives that turn into your GPS so that you can navigate, and you'll learn more on this in the next chapter. It becomes your next steps you take to create your own GPS that keeps you on track of where you're going and where you'll end up. It's the design of your own unique path which gives you the freedom to revise your path to make it more flexible and more fitting to your family needs and your schedule. You'll be able to decide and control how much you want to accomplish but always remember to keep the consistency flow of your goals.

Getting into the Action that Makes it Happen

Take the necessary action to turn your vision into a goal. Your dream is just a vision if you don't take action and that'll continue to be a reminder throughout this book. Myles Monroe said it best when he said, "there is gold in the graveyard." At first, I was puzzled. But then he said something that would not only stick with me but change my life forever. There are dreams and visions that were never able to come to life because no one acted upon them. Innovation and some of the greatest minds that never got to be heard because the action was never taken.

Fear, uncertainty, afraid someone is going to steal your invention, lack of clarity, lack of support, low self-esteem, low levels of confidence, lack of foundation and structure, poor goal setting, or one of the most common ones-not believing in yourself are all reasons to quit. We go to school to get an education only to work on someone else's dream and trade it in for our time. Chasing money on someone else's time. And still you take the risk not knowing if your position will be here today and gone tomorrow.

If you have a vision and a passion, I encourage you to take the next step and map out your goals. This next chapter will help you and show you exactly how.

CHAPTER 4

Creating Reality with Your Goals

End Goal

Setting goals that stick and become your reality are filled with endless opportunities. Especially when we look at it from an end goal perspective. Building out the vision of your future in which you desire for it to be and look like. A great technique some top leaders and athletes have used before they become successful is feel like they have already obtained their success physically and mentally. Leaders at Fortune 500 companies and small startup businesses have used this method, as well. When we know what the end goal looks like and we feel physically and mentally that we have accomplished that end goal we are preparing ourselves for the overall big success that is unique to your individual achievements. People in businesses and athletes push even harder when reaching their desired goals. Each success helped push them to achieve greater results and open the floodgates to bigger and better opportunities that were beyond their wildest dreams. From dreams to vision to your end goal let's get into how to break this system down into your own unique end goal, middle, and beginning goal that stick and become your reality.

Your end goal is your overall version of how and where you see yourself when you have accomplished everything in your vision. Notice how I said *vision* and not your life. Because we have a vision of what success looks like for where you are now. Part of this journey leads you towards a clearer structured path and destination that navigates you towards fulfilling your end goal as you learn more, gain more knowledge, while you continue to become the truest version of yourself. Your vision fits you like a glove, even when all odds seem to go against you and the distractions try to fog your direction and take you off your path.

So, keep this in mind while on your path to success. Your vision for your end goal is going to be filled with so many great accomplishments and achievements you desire for yourself. Just the thought of it gets you excited, grasping every moment to feel it just as if you are already there. This is one of the most fulfilling moments in the journey so please pause to take it all in. Know that you are deserving to feel the way you should. Feel deserving of the vision you are creating for your future because this is *your* future. I would like for you to take a couple of minutes to exercise this practice now and proceed to the next steps. So, you have taken a moment to visualize. Now it is time to get out a paper and a pencil, or on your phone, (it's where I keep my notes). Get to a comfortable place where you can write the vision you have word for word in bullet form. For example, my goals look like this.

- Multiple successful businesses
- Big house with a farm so that I can grow vegetables, and raise farm animals
- World-renowned speaker
- #1 New York Times Best Seller
- In top business magazines such as Business, Entrepreneur, Inc, Forbes etc.
- Helping millions of women globally in their business
- Helping millions of struggling families globally
- Creating a legacy that will live through many generations
- Build homes for struggling families
- Create a non-profit organization for struggling families

- Create a non-profit organization for female entrepreneurs who need funding for their startup or growing business
- Have a healthy body internally, physically, and mentally
- Travel the world to speak and learn more about history and cultures
- Create a stronger and closer relationship with my faith building a stronger foundation with God
- Build more recreational centers for children to explore their inner creative side
- Have more family reunions and get-togethers
- Meet some of the most inspiring influential people who have motivated me
- Meet different people and cultures globally
- Be fully debt-free

Yes, these are real top goals of mine! After we have stirred our creative minds, this is my real and up-to-date example of what I want my end goal to look like and feel like. I will revisit my end goal often because I can either choose to add something or take something off the list because I have accomplished it and put it in my book of memories. Now that you have it all listed out in bullets as you continue to visualize and feel your accomplishments of your end goals you are going to only take ten of these goals with you as we transition into your middle goals.

Your Top Ten Goals

Now let's take some time to look over our end goals and list them from 1-10 meaning *how many years* you think it'll take you to get there, and I will show you an example model of this. I learned this technique from researching our top leaders in the industry.

- Multiple successful businesses- 5
- Big house with a farm so that I can grow vegetables, and raise farm animals -2
- Known as a world-renowned speaker 2
- #1 New York Times Best Seller- in less than a year
- In top magazines such as Business, Entrepreneur, Inc, Forbes etc.- 1
- Helping millions of women globally in their businesses- 4
- Helping millions of struggling families globally- 4
- Creating a legacy that will live through many generations- 10
- Build homes for struggling families- 6
- Create a non-profit organization for struggling families- 1
- Create a non-profit organization for female entrepreneurs who need funding for   their startup or growing business 1

- Have a healthy body internally, physically, and mentally- (now through my entire life)
- Travel the world and learn more about history and cultures - 3
- Create a stronger and closer relationship with my faith building a stronger foundation with God- (now throughout my entire life)
- Build more recreational centers for children to explore their inner creative side- 10
- Have more family reunions and get-togethers- 2
- Meet some of the most inspiring influential people who have motivated me- 3
- Meet different people and cultures globally- 5
- Be fully debt free- 2

This isn't going to be set in stone, it's just an estimate on how long you think it'll take for you to achieve your desired end goal. Then we are going to take only ten of these goals with us to our middle goals. And guess what? The work is already done for you. You get to effortlessly continue to think about your end goal and what that looks like for you entering what your middle goals will look like for you. Take a second to look at what you have created and visualize the journey you are about to discover your new journey and experience a happier new you. Doesn't this feel exciting knowing that this is for you? Because this is what you see and feel for yourself, and you are deserving. Let's take a moment to appreciate and become grateful of your unique path you discovered for yourself. This is and will always be a part of your GPS map. No one made this up for you. This is *yours* and you should be proud of yourself and just know that I am too! Now let's dig into the next steps a little deeper and if you're anything like me, I look forward to an effortless guide.

Middle Goal

Now we are in the middle goals phase. We wrote down our end goals and visualized ourselves physically and mentally in our future end goals of how we see it in our minds unique to your individual goal. Then we wrote on the side of our goals from 1-10 determining how many years you think it will take for you to accomplish your goal. We also took a second to appreciate ourselves in the moment as you have discovered your unique journey to experience a happier new you. Now this may or may not have been something you already know. If you know it already and did this exercise with me, then I'm glad to be a part of your journey and if you did this exercise for the first time I am also glad to be a part of your journey as you learn this new technique to guide you to more opportunities in your life and business for where you are now and where you desire to be in your future.

So, let's take your top 10 goals that are closer to your 1–5-year mark and as you can see it works perfectly in our favor in this next example model. Now I want you to visualize that you have already managed and maintained these goals and enjoy the feeling. For this exercise you'll want to be in a quiet place so that you can take this entire experience in. This is something worth noting that if this exercise does not work for you the very first time do not give up on it immediately. This just means you may have too much on your mind that is distracting you and blocking your vision towards a better future for yourself. So, give this exercise a few tries and maybe even on different days, weeks, or months. Later in this book we'll talk more about the distractions and the challenges and obstacles we face and how to overcome them. After you take in this experience start writing how this journey will look for you. Ask yourself these questions:

- *How does this goal look right now in the middle of my journey towards my end goal?*
- *How does it feel and what am I experiencing in the middle of obtaining my desired goals?*
- *What are the challenges that I had to face in order to get here?*
- *What did I learn and what good habits did I pick up in the middle of my journey?*

- *Where am I physically and mentally?*
- *Am I happy with my results and proud of my accomplishments?*
- *Who helped me get here and who supported me through my journey?*
- *How grateful am I that I am achieving my wildest dreams?*
- *What opportunities did I take advantage of? (Make a list.)*

These are questions you can answer and please add your own as these questions may lead to other creative questions you may have. Now that you have explored your journey as you imagine yourself in the middle of your greatest accomplishments and goals how does this feel? Ask yourself that question and take a couple of seconds or minutes to really feel the connection between your beginning and end goal. As this becomes so real and part of your reality and becomes *of* you. Believe and trust in yourself that this is your future.

Now let's get into the next phase of narrowing our goals down into the chapter we are in now in our lives and business and how we will begin our new journey towards our new goals that are fulfilled with our desire and opportunities that will no longer have to wait on you.

Your Top Five Goals

Your top five goals are the goals you know you can accomplish within a year or two. In which we are only bringing in five for our beginning goals. It is time to narrow things down to get clear on which goal we will start on now that will get us from where we are now to where we desire to be one goal at a time. Giving you a zoomed in focus on where to start now. We came from visualizing our end goal and as we are excited and have exercised the feeling we are about to see where we will start and what that will look like for your unique path. With your pen and paper or however you decided to write your goals down we are now going to narrow our top ten goals down to our top five goals in such an effortless way.

Let's take a few minutes to narrow our top ten goals which are our long-term goals to our top five goal which we know can be accomplished in the next year or two.

Beginning Goals

We have narrowed down our long-term goals to our short-term goals and now we are narrowing our goals down to just one goal that puts you on track and flows with where you are in your life or business right now. Here are three questions to ask yourself.

- Where am I right now and how can I add this goal into my daily activities?
- Which goal will I choose out of my five goals that fits well with where I am right now?
- How will I break down my big goal into obtainable smaller objectives?

Please add some of your own questions as this list was created to inspire you to create your own questions you may have for yourself.

Navigating Your First Goal

Congratulations for making it this far into an exercise that opens up and takes a deeper dive into your goals and endless new opportunities going beyond just your goals! This is more than just a goal we are setting as we are now in our next step towards navigating your first goal. As a gentle reminder we will reflect, revisit, and sometimes revise our goals because the more we learn, the more knowledge we gain, the more we experience in life. Things tend to look a little different and our minds begin to expand. You'll start to see unique patterns of consistency while discovering new ways about ourselves. We discover growth and possibilities we have never experienced before, and our minds are now more open towards these new opportunities you have made for yourself. This is your new guide, your map, your GPS as you navigate through your daily routine. You get to make sure you're on track towards your desired destination of success and what that looks like for you. Tie your *why* into navigating your objectives to strengthen your core focus of taking action on your journey.

I'm excited for you on your new journey as it comes to you much easier than what it came for me. It took me my entire life of twenties to understand that this is how I make my dreams come true. This is how I will get and maintain the things I desire. This is how I open the floodgates to new opportunities. This is how I become the change I want to see in the world. This is how I reach my highest potential. This is how I go beyond my own limitations I put on myself.

Your Objectives are Your GPS

Last but certainly not least are the smaller objectives we will break down of the one goal you choose to navigate. Our objectives will serve us as our guide; our GPS along our journey to executing your very first goal. Let's work through this exercise together:

Your Big Goal:

- Objective 1
- Objective 2

- Objective 3
- Objective 4

Here's an example of one my Goals and the Objectives for my Goal:

My Big Goal: Starting the business I have always been passionate about

Break the big goal down into small achievable objectives keeping in mind where I am now in my journey:

- Objective 1: Create the business idea
- Objective 2: Develop the business plan
- Objective 3: Choose a business name
- Objective 4: Decide on the type of business structure
- Objective 5: Take care of all the legal tasks
- Objective 6: Start getting some ideas for the website and build the website
- Objective 7: Prepare a marketing strategy
- Objective 8: Launch my new business

You can make your objectives even more detailed, but this guide will help you stay on track. You'll also be able to create your daily to do list that helps you complete your daily tasks to navigate your Goal Preparation System.

This GPS System will ensure that even if a distraction or challenge gets in your way even if you must make an adjustment, you never stop taking action. Remember it's all about staying consistent, committed, trusting, and believing in yourself along this journey daily. And you will be sure to use the clarity model to use as a framework that keeps you on your path and to open even more new opportunities just for you.

Where You Are Now to Where You Desire to Be (A Burning Desire)

Ask yourself where you are now and write it down. Make a commitment to yourself that you will embark on your own unique journey that will lead you to your desired destination. As you completed this guide it was *you* who made it possible to paint a picture of your vision and turned it into actionable steps you can now take as your GPS guide along your journey. You are now prepared to use the Clarity Guide that will continue to shape your vision and goals as you experience a major shift into an explosion of growth, new opportunities, and a view on your life and vision at a different angle you'll enjoy navigating through.

CHAPTER 5

The Clarity Model

- Clear
- Logic
- Action
- Reflect/ Revisit/ Revise
- Improving
- Transforming
- Yourself

Welcome to The CLARITY Model Acronym Technique designed just for you to experience massive growth, open up new opportunities, bring you clarity, help you keep focus, and align you along your journey towards your biggest unique desires in your life and business. In this chapter we break that down and show you how to add this technique to your vision, your, goals, and objectives.

Here is the blueprint of the clarity model:

- **C**- Clear: *A specific clear end, middle, beginning goal objective, understanding exactly what you want*
- **L**- Logical: *The framework, steps, visualization to achieve the goal*
- **A**- Action: *Actively work on your framework, your plan, your goals and stay committed and focused*
- **R**- Reflect/ Revisit/ Revise: *Identify the gap between where you are now with your goals and where you want to be and revisit often. Revise if necessary for exponential growth*
- **I**- Improving/ Intention: *Progressing and enhancing your goals with intention for maximum achievement*
- **T**- Transforming: *Your new specific goals turned into action taking habits creating momentum that lead to your success*
- **Y**- Yourself: *Focus on where you are with your goals move towards positive changes every day and limit the distractions to achieve your goals and accelerate your path towards success*

Principle 1:C is for Clear

In the first letter and principle of the acronym is C for Clear: A specific clear end, middle, beginning goal objective, understanding exactly what you want. As we explored and navigated through these exercises in Chapter 4, first we went through what our end goal looks like and visualized ourselves being there. We took our end goal and narrowed it down from 1- 10 describing the years you think it would take to get to your desired goal. We took our goals we labeled from 1-2 years and visualized ourselves already in the middle of accomplishing our goals and choose only ten goals to paint the full picture. Then we narrowed our goals down to five goals and repeated the visualization step to narrow it down to your main goal you will start taking action on immediately and committing to consistency, trusting and believing yourself along your journey toward navigating your Clear GPS Guide. We broke down the one goal you choose into objectives that are smaller achievable goals so that even when a distraction or a challenge gets in the way you can still commit to taking daily action. This is how we get a clear bird's eye view of the goal you desire to achieve.

Principle 2: L is for Logical

The second acronym also known as the 2nd principle is L for Logical: The framework, steps, visualization to achieve the goal. This is to ensure we have a logical goal and objectives which is part of the framework you visualized in order to achieve your unique goals also discussed in Chapter 4.

Principle 3: A is for Action

Our third letter and principle 3 A is for Action: Actively work on your framework, your plan, your goals and stay committed and focused. This is one of the most important steps. If you don't take action, then nothing happens. The dream, the vision, the goal, the objectives, are all just an illusion, if you don't take action. You must take massive action on each one of your goals in order to achieve your unique desired success. You have your unique map and the steps that will navigate you along your unique journey. We are going to take daily bite sized actions and of course some days you can turn up and cover more objectives if you have a burning desire to take on more. But what is most important is that you take action, even if it is the smallest act of action.

Principle 4: Reflect/Revisit/Revise

The 4th principle the 3 R's for Reflect/ Revisit/ Revise: Identify the gap between where you are now with your goals and where you want to be and revisit often. Revise if necessary for exponential growth and to create new opportunities for your now and your future. This really has to be one of my favorite principles because here's where the magic begins–the secret lies, and the floodgates of new opportunities open just for you. Starting with the first R for Reflecting.

You will want to journal your way along your goal navigating journey so that you can also reflect not only on your goals you set, but the progress of your goals. If you can look back and see how you've progressed along your journey, then it will be exciting to see how you have gotten through some of your toughest challenges and obstacles. These are moments that are appreciated the most and motivate us in forward motion feeling and knowing that you can stand in the midst of adversity and come out on the other side of success. Reflecting also helps you with more creative thoughts and opportunities you may have not acknowledged before. Taking an extra step and going the extra mile to expand on where you were, where you are now, and we you're going in your future. Is why the next R is Revisit. You want to revisit this principle as often as possible as you get a deeper look into reflecting into your life and business within your unique goals you set that are now obtainable. Which leads us into Revise. You will experience growth, new opportunities on top of the goals you set for yourself. You'll experience and learn from the steps you took that have worked for you and the ones that didn't work for you. You'll gain tons of knowledge and open new desired paths that you'll be extremely excited about. There will be a need to tweak certain things as you navigate through your GPS, your direction toward your desired destination.

Principle 5: Improving/Intention

Coming into principle 5 I is for Improving/ Intention: Progressing and enhancing your goals with intention for maximum achievement. It's exciting to see the improvements being made right before your eyes. In the fifth principle, you are managing your goals for improvement measures. You are experiencing amazing results and you're progressing in such an effortless way. You are also intentional with the full intent of accomplishing your goals, gaining as much clarity as you possibly can, and getting further into your unique success experiencing maximum achievement.

Principle 6: Transformation

Getting into the 6th principal T for Transforming: Your new specific goals turned into action taking habits creating momentum that lead to your success. This principle is about bringing all the principles together in such a big way and discovering and being in the heart of your very own transformation. You have turned your specific goals into action taking steps, created momentum that leads to the discovery of your very own success. This is the transformation that leads, this is the transformation that prepared you for the desired transformation you longed for and executed with the abundance of principles that grounded and guided you along the way to your successful goals achieved.

Principle 7: Yourself

Last, but not least, the seventh Principle the letter Y is for Yourself: Focus on where you are with your goals move towards positive changes every day and limits the distractions to achieve your goals and accelerate your path towards success. *You* are the most important part of the principles. To see that when in preparation even if one thing seems a little off, you have a guide of principles that help you stay on track and become clear about your vision and your goals daily. As you can see, and through your experiences you know nothing happens in one day. There is no secret one-day success, especially without preparing yourself and knowing what you're looking forward to on the road to a successful destination.

You're in the driver seat of where you are going, and these principles help guide you and keep you on track turning your dreams into a vision and turning your vision into goals that become objectives pulling you into the reality of your vision. This guide has truly changed my life and not only has it changed my life. These steps were taken into careful consideration as I studied top leaders, mentors' and characteristics that lead me to a burning desire of clarity. This is in formation of unfolding clarity. I couldn't find a formula uniquely formed in easy consumable action taken steps, so I designed my own. I was inspired by the Smart Model Acronym and the work of people like James Clear, Zig Ziglar, Les Brown, Brian Tracy, Napoleon Hill, Earl Nightingale, to design my own blueprint for success. This is the Clarity Model technique that exudes new opportunities within your path beyond your desired outcomes and my intent is for you to use it to transform your own life.

CHAPTER 6

Where You Are Now to Where You Desire To Be

Let Your Vision and Goals Lead You

Your vision gives your goals direction. It will paint the bigger picture and lead you to some of your biggest goal achievements and success. Your vision helps you clearly envision your desired destination.

When you have a clear vision, it's easier to set and achieve specific goals. Your vision can help guide you through tough decisions and keep you motivated when obstacles arise.

If you're not sure where to start, sit down and brainstorm what you want your life or business to look like in the future. What are your long-term goals? How can you turn your dreams into reality? Answering these questions will help get you started on creating a *Vision Board*. This is a powerful tool that can help keep you focused on your goals and vision.

Remember, your Vision is what will lead you to success! So, keep it at the forefront of your mind as you work towards your goals. Let it be your guide and watch as you achieve great things!

As you move along in your journey, let your vision and goals lead you. With guidance of the CLARITY technique, continue to follow this model to lead you through your business model for years to come. The further and further away you get from whether it be your business model, plan, life, mission–the less chance you have of succeeding. Some of the most profound leaders know the importance of making sure they are crystal clear about their next steps in their business now and in their future. Businesses fail when they get further and further away from their specific goal. Most of the time, their goals are not written out and they're not taking advantage of the many opportunities they have by revisiting, revising, and reflecting daily or weekly on where they are with their business plans then, now, and in their future. The beauty in letting your goals and vision lead you, is that it becomes your clear guide for your now unfolding into your future. Your guide becomes effortless because it becomes one within you. You are becoming daily. You are learning daily; you are gaining knowledge daily. You are revising your goals, your vision, your action plan and the more you reflect the more you start noticing the things normally someone else would tell you. You become more self-aware and understanding of the next steps you need to take in your business. This is all a part of charting your course and leading yourself towards your desired destination effortlessly, because it shouldn't always be hard.

Faith is Your Foundation

As you let your vision and goals lead you, the key to strengthening your journey is to have a solid foundation built with faith. When you have faith in something, it provides a strong foundation for you to stand on. No matter what challenges or obstacles you face in life, your faith will always be there to support you. It's like a rock that you can always rely on, no matter what.

If you don't have faith in anything, then you're constantly searching for something to believe in. This can leave you feeling lost and confused, because you don't have anything solid to hold onto. Faith is what gives you a sense of direction and purpose in life. It's what helps you get through tough times and come out stronger on the other side.

When you have faith, you're never alone. You always have something to believe in, even when things are tough.

Faith is the light that guides you through the darkness. It's the hope that keeps you going when everything else seems hopeless.

Faith is your foundation. It's what you build your life on. It's what gives you strength when you're weak, and hope when you're lost. Never lose faith in yourself, or in the things that you believe in. Remember, faith is your foundation. You must believe in yourself as well as believe in wherever your faith lies.

> *"If you don't believe in yourself then why should anyone else believe in you?"*
>
> -MYLES MUNROE

This quote shifted my paradigm and perspective for me. Faith is always your foundation. It's what helps build a strong standing home for everything you need to start, manage, vision, and take action. Whether you're on stage or building your dream community faith is your foundation. It is what keeps you going strong even when it feels as though everything is crumbling right before your eyes. We have all experienced that feeling of disappointment. It's happened to me several times in my business and to be quite honest those days felt like the end of me.

But it's in those moments where I have also learned my biggest lessons as I let my faith lead and guide me. No, we cannot control all the circumstances that are a part of our journey, but the key is to learn how to manage the ones you didn't factor in. It's also important for you to manage your emotions, attitude, and thoughts so that you can focus more on the circumstances you choose rather, than the ones you didn't choose for yourself and have patience. Faith is the structure that holds it all together like glue. Before you know it, you will have a place where you can call home.

> *"Lay one brick at a time as perfectly as you can*
> *and soon you will have a wall."*

> -WILL SMITH

Check In with Yourself

Where are you now physically and mentally? It's an important question to ask yourself. Maybe there are some debts that are holding you back from living the free life you feel that you deserve. So, both physically and mentally it can be draining. Your attention to your goals may seem so far away when there seem to be more important things that need to be addressed and taken care of in your life.

One good exercise to do is to write down all the things that are taking up all your time, your energy, and your mental and physical ability to have a peace of mind. Go into detail and write down how much you owe and then break down how much you can pay each month towards the depth. Paying something versus paying nothing makes all the difference. At times it could be family members that have you in a string tie and that can be physically and mentally draining. Being honest with yourself and your family members is important. Whether it's a get- together and you can't attend or money you can't lend at this very moment, a simple *no* is enough.

So where are you now in your process? You can go as far as writing it down and creating even more questions in curiosity. Curiosity can lead you to bigger and better places. Your mental and physical state is important to identify along your journey. It's like going on your regular checkup. Check in with yourself often and make sure you are good physically and mentally.

After all, you help many people and although it's great to help people we can forget about ourselves sometimes. To give your family, friends, clients, or customers the best version of yourself you have to make sure your taking care of yourself. I am guilty of this myself and I'm sure lots of us are nodding our heads right now as we can all relate. Sometimes you need a day or two to relax and other times you just need a seven-day vacation to bring you back to reality.

Taking some time for yourself can lead to some of your most creative moments. I took some time away from this book within the challenge I created for myself. The challenge was to finish this book in twelve days. I am now approaching the deadline very quickly but within those twelve days I had to take a break. Words started to look the same and sound the same. So, I took a step back and when the time was right, I came back to it and finished it.

Of course, this was a challenge, so I held myself to my deadline still just to build trust and commitment within myself. Trusting myself and knowing I could do something that looked far beyond my reach and of course a challenge that is rare for a majority of people. So, my point is to take some time for yourself for a healthy state of mind. This way, if a distraction or something overwhelming comes your way you can be in a much more relaxed state of mind. You'll have more patience to take on the next challenge or obstacles that comes your way without warning.

Where You Desire to Be is Where You Should Be

Where you desire to be is exactly where you *should* be. Affirm it, have faith, believe it, and trust yourself. There is a such thing as your intuition. I believe that your intuition and your faith work together as a team. Your clarity of goals and vision map is your inspiration, and you should be dedicated to the journey and the destination. After all its where you desire to be. No one told you to go there.

You had a vision and you mapped out what it will take to get to your desired place which is where you should be. Taking massive action is important but again if you have your goals mapped out and you're reflecting, revising, and revisiting your masterplan the more likely you will become aware of what you need. You start to realize the importance of taking massive action that contributes in an effortless way.

I love an effortless process, but in order to get there, you must do the hard work first just like anything else you start. But doing it for yourself is so much more rewarding. Where you desire to be is where you *should be,* and you shouldn't let anyone tell you anything different. Sometimes people don't really know or think that you can accomplish things that may seem far to them but not so much for you. What's obtainable for you may not look as attainable for them.

That's OK because we are all built differently, and you are your own unique person. Now once you get where you desire to be it shouldn't end there and that's the exact reason why you continue to reflect, revise and revisit so that you can make your vision for your future even stronger because you become wiser, educated, aligned, reaching higher heights and thresholds within yourself. You should always be in competition with yourself, and you should always be striving to become an even better person than what you were yesterday, and, in this case, you are doing this in such a positive healthy way.

Protecting Your Why, Your Passion, Your Joy

Protect your why, your passion and your joy. These three things that are part of your foundation can get buried within the distraction, challenges, and obstacles. You must always keep this in front of you. Keep it in a place you report to daily. I keep these thoughts in my notes of my phone because I journal daily. So, figure out where that place may be for you. Protect the reason *why* you work so hard to go after your goals. If you don't, something else will come in and reconstruct or reconfigure your why. By the time you know it *your why* will continue to come last in your mind.

This is another reason why so few in the world accomplish their goals. Be one of the few who is focused, no matter what distractions or unforeseen event comes forth. Don't let anything knock you off your track. Everyone experiences the rocky roads of starting on their goal, starting a business, or growing a business. The key is not to let anyone, or anything get you off your charted course no matter what, which takes discipline and consistency.

Trust your process and continue to gain knowledge that will help you get further along your journey. Protect your passion, it's the life of everything you started. Losing site of your passion leads to emptiness, giving up too soon, and so many missed opportunities. Keep your passion alive and in front of you to build a long-lasting connection that will not only inspire your journey it will also inspire others around you or in your community. Protecting your joy is extremely important. Sometimes it can be hard, appreciation and gratitude can take you so far. I like to add appreciation and gratitude daily it brings me joy and happiness even when things can get a little overwhelming. Protect your passion and your joy and continue building your gratitude because these will all help you along your journey towards success.

CHAPTER 7

Reaching Beyond Your Limitations

Positive and Negative Self-Talk

Those negative thoughts are very potent and so are those positive ones. Negative thoughts can lead you to some of your darkest moments. A negative mindset will stop you from pursuing your wildest dreams and accomplishing big goals your more than capable of accomplishing. I didn't realize how negative my mindset was until I heard Oprah speaking about our thoughts and our goals.

> *"One of the biggest keys to success is having a positive mindset."*
>
> -OPRAH WINFREY

You might feel like I did when I first heard this quote. I thought exactly what anyone else would think going through challenging times. *How, when I'm struggling – there's nothing else I can do about my situation, but think negative?* I had a fixed mindset, and it was very crippling in almost every area in my life. But when I heard Oprah say it for the first time that was also the first seed that was planted within me. Deep down inside I wanted to experience change. I wanted to improve, I wanted to be more positive-minded, and I wanted to know what success felt like. I wanted to experience it the way I saw it in my dreams and my vision. There was only one problem, I didn't know where to start.

Eventually I found it day by day year by year. Positivity took time and patience, and self-improvement came overtime. Replacing the negative mindset with a healthy positive mindset wasn't easy, but I wish I had done it sooner. I'm in such a better place with myself and my mind. It's a level of success you hold within yourself and a sense of accomplishment that makes you feel incredible, and it spreads like wildfire. Practicing self-development is very important on your journey towards getting the things you desire in your life and business. After all, you also must be able to help others along your journey. It's one of the greatest feelings when you get to help someone, and they tell you how much you've helped them get the clarity, focus and alignment along their journey. There was a time where getting on the right track for me seemed so far away with the wrong mindset. Now, I get to help others find their right track and develop the right mindset to get the things they desire to have.

"In a growth mindset, challenges are exciting rather than threatening. So rather than thinking, oh, I'm going to reveal my weakness, you say, oh wow, here's a chance to grow."

-CAROL DWECK

Having a Growth Mindset

There is the fixed mindset and the growth mindset. Those with a fixed mindset believe their intelligence, talents and personalities are fixed traits that cannot change. They believe we are born with a certain level of ability (or special skills), that we are unable to improve our level of abilities over time.

A growth mindset describes a way of viewing challenges and setbacks. People who have a growth mindset believe that even if they struggle with certain skills, their abilities aren't set in stone. They think that with work, their skills can improve over time.

A Long-Distance Relationship with Yourself

Who am I? I despised the fact that someone could even say *I know you better than you know yourself*. I thought that was creepy, impossible, and a way to control and manipulate someone. I quickly identified that I needed to get to know myself better than what I had known. I needed to build a heathy relationship with my inner and outer self. Doing this with three children and a husband wasn't easy, but it was worth my sanity, the next chapter of life I was entering, and my desire and will to get connected with myself on a deeper level. At first it was weird to me because I was always told don't do certain things like don't talk to yourself, don't answer yourself. And to me it started to sound and look like I couldn't have a relationship with myself. I had created a long-distance relationship with myself.

A lot of us have a long-distance relationship with ourselves and we don't realize it. We want to know more about someone else's problems, and issues more than we want to know about our own which is a cause of distraction. It's almost like it's normalized to know more about someone else than your own self. I used to listen to music every day depending on the different emotions within myself. This didn't fix my problem this took my mind off the problem and as soon as I stopped listening to the music my problems, sure enough, were still there waiting on me.

The more I became serious about my business, the more I became serious about my life and about the choices I was making and the habits I had created for myself over time. I felt the urge to improve and become a better version of myself to go into a different chapter in my life. I had a visual of what I knew my highest potential and capabilities where. I was ready to take those limitations off myself and rise above me standing in my own way. Once again, day by day year by year got me closer to a better version of myself and it was something to be both humble and proud about. Know yourself and build a relationship and a bond with yourself no one or nothing can break.

Going Beyond Your Limitations

"Self-confidence is really self-trust."

- ED MYLETT

Go beyond your limitations and you'll be surprised where you end up. Rather than telling yourself it's impossible, tell yourself it is possible, prepare yourself as best you can, and take action. Learn the ups the downs and everything in between. Take risks on yourself and trust your intuition and your burning desire. You can either let your limitations guide you into putting yourself in a cage or living a life filled with opportunities. Going beyond your limitations gives you a plethora of new opportunities and a way to see things in a new light. If you want to grow, you have to identify the limitations you set for yourself that hold you back from becoming the unique person you see yourself becoming. Sometimes you're not aware of the set-back.

Awareness helps you identify the blind spots. You are unique and you have a very creative mind, and you deserve the things you desire to have in life, so go for your biggest goal. You never know where it may lead you. You'll always have one more to give, one more thing you can do to make a change and the will to make a difference, the power of one more. You'll always have the power of one more in you even when you feel as though you want to give up.

CHAPTER 8

Life and Business

How to Use the CLARITY Model in Your Life and Business

The CLARITY model can be used for both your life and your business goals. It can be used for your life when things seem confusing and unclear due to unforeseen events, distractions holding you back from getting to your biggest goals you look forward to accomplishing in your life. The CLARITY model can also be used for your business when there's too much clutter and things seem to get blurry taking you further and further away from your *why* that you had when you started your business. You can use the CLARITY technique in many ways. Here are six ways to start:

1. Find a deeper connection with your purpose.
2. Take responsibility when you get off track.

3. Take action every day.
4. Create empowering habits.
5. Create unlimited new opportunities.
6. Tap into unlimited growth potential with in yourself.

Let's get a little deeper into how we can use clarity in these six ways. Using the clarity method technique to help you have a deeper connection with your purpose can lead you to the success you desire to have. Whether it be something you've been dreaming of for years, or you're just figuring it all out. With everything that goes on in our lives and business daily, it's very easy to get further and further away from your purpose without noticing it. Discover your true needs and focus on what you have in front of you.

Two, it helps you hold yourself responsible and accountable when you get off track in your life and business. You'll notice that with your efforts, things get better and without any effort at all nothing happens. When you want it bad enough, you take the extra step even when all seems impossible. You start to get a sense of responsibility as you hold yourself accountable to do what needs to be done now and what can be done at a different level of higher intent. Three is to take action every day.

Consistency is key and the momentum you create will help you continue to cultivate your focus and commitment. You'll start to see a pattern and you'll see the growth in you. That is the most exciting rewarding thing–to be aware of and to see your efforts come to reality. Four, create empowering habits that make you want to keep going and become unstoppable. Creating habits that will keep you moving forward and not backwards. You'll see yourself using Reflect, Revisit and Revise often. It's what helps you get deeper into the habit. Applying the same method in many ways that work for you is the goal! That's why this step is important and is not to be missed. Five, create new opportunities as you'll see through this book unlimited opportunities are truly what you will receive. You will continue to follow your true path and direction. It's *yours* and you get to decide. Last, but not least, *know and trust* that it's all possible and let the flow of this technique take you beyond the unthinkable.

Your Intentions

Take action with intention and focus. When you aim at nothing, then there's nothing to be intentional about and your focus will be limited. Do what you're passionate about with intention and you'll go far bringing all these components together. Move through the start of your day till the end of your day with full intent of taking all prepared action. Focus on what you're doing and minimize distractions. Remember that even with the distractions and circumstances that aren't of your own making, you'll be able to see clearly. You'll be able to navigate through the uncertainty in a stress-free way. Being able to manage circumstances that you didn't create is important. There are times where many of us have taken the wrong route and decided to focus on the wrong circumstances. It's important to focus and be intentional on the circumstances you created for yourself rather than the latter. Be intentional even with the affirmations you create for yourself and say them daily. I know you've heard of the tongue being very powerful. Use it in the most positive way as it is extremely powerful. Don't be afraid to do the difficult things. Remember, we are being intentional. Shift any limiting beliefs that may hold you back from the success you're aiming for.

Can you really balance life and business?

I believe that life and business can have a great relationship or a bad relationship. I'll share five ways you can balance the two, but they will only work if your intentional about it.

- What is important in your life: spend some time thinking about your values and what's important to you.

- Time Management: Practice time management.
- Have set boundaries: When you're at work be intentional about working.

Knowing what works in your environment and what doesn't work in your environment. Do the same for your life. Sometimes it can be hard to turn work off when you're supposed to be on vacation, visiting family, having a spa day or a day to yourself and this can also be in reverse. At work thinking about a vacation or being elsewhere. My opinion I don't think this is all bad it's when you do it all the time and you don't have a laser bird's eye view focus. So have boundaries in place so that you can enjoy both and look forward to the next best thing.

- Focus on outcomes and impact. Put in your best effort and communicate it, and it will be noticed. It's not only about how many items you cross off a to-do list but also how they relate to the bigger picture. Focusing on impact will help you prioritize your time in the best way possible. Set clear goals or a schedule for yourself if that helps you stay organized. There will always be more work but organizing your time will give you the time you need to dedicate to activities and goals outside of work. In the best way put, focus on outcomes and impact.

- Stick to a daily routine: Take a full week to note what some of your daily practices and habits are. In them you'll find what's most important to you, what your core focus is, and on the flip side, realize some things that take up too much of your time. Continue to revisit, reflect, and revise to fine tune what you want your life and business to look and feel like. You can have the things you want in life how you see it.

- Accountability - When strolling through life and business obtaining our goals and getting to the place we desire to be, we learn some things along the way about ourselves. Sometimes we mess up, we make some choices that don't serve us well. Making some decisions that cost us our time while making some wrong turns that eventually teach us our most valuable lessons.

Life is like going through an obstacle course. It's important to note that as you experience rough terrains that you hold yourself accountable whether the accountability aims at the tough times or in times that need to be acknowledged so that you can move forward with a better attitude along your journey. Attitude is another important aspect of attaining the goal you have set in your vision. There are going to be things and people that come, go, and stick around and closely identifying who you are and what you do in the process is important to your next steps. It's all a learning process and there are always areas in our lives where we can grow and learn from.

CHAPTER 9

Charting Your Course with the GPS Model

Your Journey

It's the journey that leads to exciting places. Focus on the journey. When I started focusing on the journey more, then my mind became calm. I was able to stop and feel myself breathe in breaths of fresh air. Certain things I hadn't noticed before became noticeable. The smaller things in life mattered. It's all a part of the journey and it's worth writing it all down so that you can see some of your best moments unfold with clarity. Success is in your unique journey you charted. The everyday chiseling and carving out your clear path working through each step. Choose to start and don't give up even when the odds seem like they're against you. Keep pushing through the next steps, the objectives you set in place for your goals. Keeping your vision and goals at the top of your mind daily is a motivation tactic. Everything you do daily is a contribution to the scaling up and getting closer and closer to your vision. Even when it feels like you have failed, instead look at it as a learning curve and that you can try again until you find what works for you. It's the reason why every success story is different, and everyone has a different journey to embark on. Not one person walks the same journey because we are all unique in our direction and path.

Preparation is Key

Preparation is the secret to opening the doors to new opportunities. You can never be too prepared, and I'll tell you why. The lack of preparation leads to making decisions that are not only hard to make but end up costing you more in life or business. Lack of preparation leads to missed opportunities and poor performance. "By failing to prepare, you are preparing to fail." Being prepared can reduce fear, anxiety, overwhelm, and doubt. In your life and business, you'll experience growth through different seasons of your journey. You'll learn through the failures, and you'll learn through your greatest achievements. Preparing your next steps helps you expand on greater levels of creativity, especially in business.

You may have prepared your one-year business plan, and something shifted in the economy. This is where going back to your one-year business plan to brainstorm puts you at a better advantage. You can go back to your business plan and see where you can pivot. Being prepared isn't just about being prepared in the moment or just in your mind because you think you may know what to do next. Being prepared is also having that one-year, five-year, ten-year life, or business plan. You'll want to use the 3 Rs from the CLARITY technique Reflect, Revisit, Revise daily, weekly, monthly, and yearly. As you manage yourself through preparation, you'll start to see so many things that will work for you effortlessly.

The Opportunity

Preparation puts you on track for new opportunities in an effortless way. When you can see it in your favor and see how it can work for you in that moment is when it looks and feels like the greatest opportunity. No matter if it's big or small. It's when you cannot see the opportunities that are already here for you to take advantage of that you miss. Losing out on an opportunity looks more like a foolish thing to consider and is equivalent to taking the wrong risk.

In life, you're taking a risk every single day. As the same goes for your business. But what if we knew that we were closer to taking the *right risk* rather taking the *riskier risk*? It's all in the opportunity that you can see. For example, the CLARITY model technique is an opportunity. An opportunity to use a system that will help you with your steps to getting what you desire to have. You are being observant of your now and your future and preparing for the best. To aim and hit those goals and objectives, you set the goal to form into your reality. That's a huge opportunity filled with systems that are preparing you for your big win. So go for it and give it your all. You'll start off small to get momentum and build the consistency that will give you more than what you ever dreamed of.

An Attitude of Gratitude

Gratitude is an open room that leads to an abundance of happiness. Gratitude is one of many positive emotions. It truly is and there is enough of it for everyone in such a big world. It's all in your positive actions. You feel grateful when you experience gratitude from something big or small in your life. You respond with the feeling of kindness and generosity. Gratitude helps you deal with adversity no matter what you go through.

"A heart of gratitude is humble in praise."

- PSALMS 51:17

It's perfectly normal to want more and to have more but knowing what you have now and being grateful for just that in this very moment is important. Because in each one of those things there is meaning and purpose of it. Gratitude could be the very thing that leads you to your desired destination.

Appreciating What You Have

Appreciate what you have–both the big things and the small things. Because even the small things like a small seed of faith gives you the courage to believe and the appreciation to have a vision that leads you to your desired steps that navigate you towards what you desire. Appreciation and gratitude work hand and hand. There is a special feeling that sparks within when you're aware of how much appreciation you have for life itself. As there is so much to be grateful and appreciative for. Appreciation makes you feel valued and drives you to do your very best. This path that you are taking, the goals you are setting, and the objectives that will get you to where you want to be will help you look forward to a new path and it's something to be appreciative and excited about.

The GPS Goals Preparation System

The goals preparation system is what helps you keep track of your next steps. You can go to https://clarityofgoalsandvision.com and get your Clarity GPS journal. The goal preparation process is one of the most important steps–you don't want to miss when seeking clarity for your goals. There are many journals you can use, but the Clarity GPS journal focuses on your goal, preparation, weekly accomplishments, your growth, opportunities now and your future–helping you keep a stable track record of where you are along your journey right now. It helps you to see your highest potential, overcome self-doubt, have clarity, and less doubt. Be confident about where you're going and where you're taking yourself. You want to do something you're passionate about and you put your all into it for the first week. Your first week will show you exactly what you're doing, and you'll be able to come up with many ways to push the envelope or try something you think could work even better as you plan. You start to become incredibly creative. So, if you don't know how you're going to start something, don't worry, just start to record your week and your *how* will begin to reveal itself.

CHAPTER 10

Clarity Does Not Strike; It Unfolds

Clarity Does Not Strike (No Overnight Action)

C larity does not strike over night. There are a series of events that take place with aim and focus. Clarity isn't some magical word that sets in automation mode like the world of technology we live in. The more and more we use technology, and we have a need of technology, everything may seem automated. But if you look in a little closer only certain things can be automated. For example, certain tasks in your business can be automated, but your business and marketing plan you created word for word cannot be automated. Those two things came from your unique vision and over time you turned it into a business. The reason why you started is wildly important. But with time came clarity on how you would strategically start and grow your business with the use of many creative automated tools that are available for anyone to use today.

Getting clarity is no overnight magical bliss, but when you receive it, it will feel so magical. You'll forget the challenges and obstacles it took for you to get here. It's an amazing feeling and an all-time high that's worth the entire journey walking into your own unique clarity.

Clarity Unfolds (One Step at a Time)

Clarity unfolds right before your eyes and your life. And you deserve to see it unfold as you continue along your journey taking it one step at a time. You start to see things you couldn't see before, and the details become highlighted. Give yourself grace. We wish to have the things we want overnight, but to have it all and not know why you have it, will go to waste very quickly. Clarity unfolds and the more you get in tuned and connected to your daily actions and get focused on your unique clarity over time it will unfold, and you'll be glad you waited.

It's just like this book. I wanted to write it in the beginning of 2022 but for some reason I couldn't sit down long enough to finish it. My intention was to continue writing this book and slowly but surely, I moved away from the consistency and flow I once had. One thing that stood out the most was that I couldn't connect with the words I was writing. I started something and I felt so guilty that I didn't continue and now I'm glad I took more time to unfold the clarity and time I needed.

If it weren't for me journaling my life and business, I would have never been clearer today and knowing the reason why I didn't have a clear mindset. Two words: experience and growth. What I experienced this year was amazing. I learned so much just this year alone journaling, I was able to gain so much clarity and growth. I'm grateful that I got to share with amazing people who have read this book and who follow my journey.

Accumulation (Repetitive Actions)

Repetitive actions are the accumulation of a clear result when you aim at something specific. We aim at our goals by writing them down mapping out your objectives and setting up your Goal Preparation System GPS. Over time you will accumulate and gather resourceful information about your journey with what works and what doesn't work. Of course, you'll want to be intentional about what does work and increase the things that are working out for you.

How You Know When You Need Clarity

You'll know you need clarity when you feel empty inside and you feel like you could do more. You have a burning desire to fulfill your passion. You have a vision, and you need to know your next steps. You have goals you desire to accomplish. Or you feel like you've done it all and taking a clarity walk could put you back on track. You may feel misunderstood, and no one understands you. Lacking balance in life and business. Starting a business or growing your business you'll need intentional focus, clarity, techniques, and systems to guide you along a successful path. Opening up defined clarity in your life will help you see what you truly need to really focus on. Create space in your mind so that you can process and identify what really matters. Keep a clear mind and clear thoughts when seeking clarity. When you don't have clarity, you have lots of uncertainty that leads to confusion. Build, create, and get closer to the clear state of mind you need and chart your course.

In Desperate Need of a Little Transformation

You may feel at times you are in desperate need of a little transformation. You want to go further. You want that freedom you've been imagining for yourself and your family. You want more unlimited options and the things you can and want to do. You want a specific type of lifestyle. Or you want to be able to control your time by building the business you're passionate about. You're in desperate need of a transformation that you want in order to turn your life around. Keep in mind the transformation isn't always glamorous and you'll have to be ready for some bumps, some fails, some wins, and some success. You can choose to make it fun, while learning, educating yourself, and discovering new things about yourself and the journey. It's all in the process and where you are leading yourself.

We Don't Talk About Clarity Enough (in the Struggle)

There can be struggle in clarity when you're doing it alone with no one and not a thing in sight to help you get to where you desire to be. It took me forever to get to the books to help and show me because I did not have the support to go in the direction. I decided to take on this journey myself. I had to learn and educate myself so that I could get to where I wanted to be. So it wasn't that I didn't have the support–because I did, I just didn't have that specific support to take me towards the direction I desired to walk in. I was willing to go at it alone in the beginning and trusted the *how* would come later.

I depended on my faith to be my foundation and I don't think God would have had it any other way. I was guided through faith. As I got a little deeper into my journey, I would have visions and inspiration of my next course of action. That's when I discovered systems that would guide me in the path I'm on today. I couldn't be more elated to share it with the world and lead others to clarity. I struggled along the way; I stumbled along the way with doubts and times when things got overwhelming.

I spent day in and day out researching clarity, even with managing my existing business and building something that I knew in my heart I was passionate about. I didn't know how I would get from where I was to where I wanted to be but along the journey one day at a time the message was getting clearer each time. I learned so much and educated myself so much that I almost got stuck there because I became too comfortable.

I needed to start taking action and get uncomfortable. Another area of struggle that would take time and that's the beauty of the journey. I started to chart my journey in my journal because I knew it would be important for me to reflect, revisit and revise my steps. I needed to be aware of my actions and what was stopping me that maybe I couldn't see from the surface level.

I'm very detailed but I became even more detailed when I started to journal every single day. I started to see some patterns of good and bad habits and I was excited to start working on what I could work in next. I even started hiring new people for my business and charted that course and was able to determine if I needed to continue to work with them or not. I liked journaling, writing it all down, building systems and techniques that worked for me through inspiration from top leaders was my guide. I turned my struggle into a system for finding clarity that worked for me and now I'm sharing it with you.

CHAPTER 11

Challenges Female Entrepreneurs Face

How to Overcome the Distractions, Challenges, Overwhelm

Is there a proven way to overcome distractions, challenges, and overwhelm that happen in our lives and in our business? I believe there is a way, but we are not perfect. Instead, we can strive for excellence for better performance.

Distractions come knocking at your door daily, you can identify some of them but other times we feel obligated to the distraction. At times you can't just walk away from them, but you can manage the circumstances, manage time, and be more productive.

Just When You Thought You Had It

Things were going great until...... I had it until...... just when I thought I had it I .... Finish the sentence because it's the last time you'll hear yourself saying it once you're done with this book and you put all the guides, techniques, and systems into action. *But how do I get my vision from vision to reality?* There are steps that you'll take to get to the how. As a matter of fact, everything you're doing now is all a part of the how. Everything you do is the how and has a direct result. You will discover the even bigger how.

The Secret to Having Clear Thoughts

The secret to having clear thoughts takes time. You'll need to clear your mind that was once filled with negativity. You'll need to break the negativity barriers and pour in all positive thoughts. You can add this to your daily habits starting with just five minutes of your time daily.

Preferably you'll start doing this in the morning because it's when you have time for yourself and a quiet mind. My first attempt at this was like most, when I tried this for the first time. It felt very chaotic because I didn't know how to focus on one thing and control my focus there. I had a wandering mind and I had to figure out how to get it to focus. I worked hard at it and no it didn't take a couple of days and it didn't take a couple of weeks it took more than a few weeks. I was determined because with my wandering thoughts I didn't have a clear focus on what it was that I actually wanted.

Focus

Let's get in tune with focus. It's a powerful thing to have. The more focus, the more you gain. Getting focused on having clarity of your vision and then turning it into your unique goal is the first step. This turns into your reality because you focused on one goal that led you to performing daily habits and then that gave you the results you desired to have. And yes, I said *daily*. Even if you must take that goal and minimize it a couple of days in that week, it's your consistency you commit to daily that matters. A zoned in focus.

Of course, life keeps happening, but soon that goal turns into that vision, and this turns into your reality. Your focus leads to new opportunities and a more creative mind. It's easy to get caught up and focused on what everyone else is doing. This is a huge distraction in and of itself. When you see so many people doing some of the same things it's easy to tell yourself to trust the process because everyone else is doing it. Trust that you have your own uniqueness and if you strongly feel like your direction, you see yourself going on is slightly different, then chart that course. No one can be you; you are your own version of clarity.

Alignment

Alignment is a part of the results you'll get from taking action throughout this book. From clarity of your vision to clarity of your goals and discovering the results in an authentic way. There is no need to be overwhelmed about the process everything becomes effortless as things in your life and business forms and become more aligned in a meaningful way. Your goals help keep you aligned and moving forward to your next objective.

The Constant Reminder

To achieve the things that you want in life, you need to give yourself the constant reminder revisiting your goals, your vision, your journal, your thoughts that align with the current circumstances you set for yourself. This is what your road to self-achievement looks like. Once you know what you need to do to get the things you want and desire you learn how to continue moving forward. It's easy to forget what you want or push things back and say *I'll get to it later.* Then later never comes and you don't bother to remind yourself of the importance of that objective. Maybe someday years from now you decide to remind yourself of the track you could have been on had certain circumstances not interrupted your schedule. Bring yourself out of these thought patterns and adjust to new ways that will help you overcome this mindset. That constant reminder leads to lifelong learning and education and is a life changing discovery.

A Life-changing Discovery

Having clarity in your life leads to a life changing discovery. Along the journey you will find, create, progress, and challenge yourself to go even further once you gain your momentum and you start to see the results you contributed today in and day out. Taking action comes with big rewards. The more action you take, of course the bigger the reward. Your vision will start to take flight so trust and believe your path. You'll be glad you did.

CHAPTER 12

The Secret Clarity Effect

The opposite of clarity

What is the opposite of clarity? Obscurity and vagueness. This book is the opposite of these two words. Clarity can't be reached if you're at surface level capacity. Surface level capacity makes us too comfortable. Getting clarity is going beneath the surface and going deeper into our lives and business with the willingness to understand that every day truly adds up. Reflect, revisit, and revise daily.

The Clarity Cause and Effect

Let's look at the cause and effect of clarity a little deeper. The cause is clarity, and the effect of clarity is getting from where you are now to where you desire to be. Our next book you'll see in 2023. By the time you read this book, either that book is being written, or it's already out. Cause and effect play an important role in the universe. Clarity makes it possible for your vision to become your reality. The cause and effect of having clarity is to have a clear mind. Being able to see your clearest thoughts and path in front of you. The cause of applying the clarity technique is having a proven technique that helps you get through some of your most toughest times staying on track with your goals. Sticking to your values and always in control of your circumstances. The effect that the clarity effect has on each individual who applies the technique is clarity of your journey and direction. Opening up a world of new opportunities and possibilities that awaken on the other side of your biggest desires.

The simple law of cause and effect

Change your actions, and you change your life… Transform your thoughts, and you will create a brand-new destiny.

The law of cause-and-effect states that:

- Every effect has a specific and predictable cause.
- Every cause or action has a specific and predictable effect.

This means that everything that we currently have in our lives is an effect that is a result of a specific cause.

Success is created within you.

Creating the conditions and circumstances of your life and manifesting your future in front of your eyes. In fact, how you react to the events, people, and circumstances in your life, is actually determining by how you feel on a daily basis — creating a chain of effects that are constantly transforming your destiny anew every day.

Your thoughts are creatively manifesting your reality.

Your life experience is a reflection of thought manifestations.

It is never too late to turn things around.

And gain greater clarity about your life and thought processes.

What will you do to gain clarity today?

Further Questions

- How can I begin interpreting my world differently?
- How can I change my patterns of thinking?
    - How can I model other successful people's behaviors, habits, decisions, thoughts, and actions to improve my own life?

CONCLUSION

When I started writing this book, I had a vision for what I wanted to happen. There was a mission to be fulfilled, and I was going to be the one to discover the meaning of Clarity, even if it took me a lifetime. Not only did I find Clarity for myself, but my mission has also grown, and my passion is helping my fellow female entrepreneurs find their unique success through navigating their direction in life and business. Thank you for reading this book–for talking about this book with your family and friends. Thank you for sharing it with recent graduates and those starting or changing careers. You are all part of this journey with me, and I appreciate you.

ACKNOWLEDGEMENTS

I wrote this book with a burning desire to write every word in it while my husband and I were renovating a beautiful home. During the process of creating this book there are many close people I would like to thank. I would first like to thank my husband Eric Jasper for playing every role while standing right by my side every step of the way as I wrote this book. Without him I wouldn't have had the freedom to write and think some of my clearest thoughts while putting words and chapters together whether it was on paper, my phone, or my laptop. He truly gave me peace of mind in the process of bringing this book to life. I love you!

Secondly, I am forever grateful for my children. Izabella, Felisity, and Xzelexton for encouraging, supporting, and giving me a peace of mind. I am overwhelmed with grace and appreciation from the start to the finish of this book wanting to know every detail and how they could help me! I want them to know that mommy has a heart filled with endless love for them and their support means everything to me.

Third I would like to thank a special someone who is close to me and helped me hold myself accountable while reaching the deadline to my manuscript. My sister Serenity Bowe. I would also like to thank my mom for encouraging and uplifting me from the very beginning.

I'd like to give a big thank you to my editor Anna Kline for turning my rough draft into a tight enjoyable easy to read manuscript. From the start she loved the concept of the book and was excited to be a part of the experience.

Many thanks to all the family members and friends who kept an update of the book and ready to receive their first copy.

Finally, I want to thank you for reading this book. I am forever grateful for the opportunity, the experience, and the journey.

ABOUT THE AUTHOR

S antima Jasper is an author, business coach, business leader, and entrepreneur focused on clarity of vision, goals, and direction in life and business.

No matter the vision, goal, or dream clarity of goals and vision offers a 7-step proven framework to navigate a clear path and direction in your life and business. Santima Jasper focuses on clarity. One of the first steps when you are starting anything. You have to have a clear vision, clear thoughts, and a clear path to start navigating the direction you see yourself going now and, in the future, you desire to have. She reveals the strategy that gets you started now and as you continue unfolding clarity along your journey.

Clarity does not strike it unfolds. If you're having trouble with articulating, clear thoughts to help you paint that clear picture clarity of goals and vision guides you through frameworks that keep you focused and aligned on your path.

Whether you are just starting, or your 10-year plan isn't going as planned just as you pictured it. The techniques and tools provided in this book will bring you clarity, focus, and alignment eliminating uncertainty, lack of clarity, and doubts.

During over a decade in her entrepreneurship journey Santima Jasper faced a significant amount of adversity in a male dominant industry. Santima now owns several other successful businesses she founded and runs today as CEO. She has impacted thousands of people donating her resources such as workbooks, courses, and speaking at schools and workshops for self and professional development. Santima Jasper is committed to this journey along with her bigger purpose and passion to share her techniques and strategies worldwide to millions of people across the globe.

https://clarityofgoalsandvision.com

INDEX

CLARITY OF GOALS AND VISION

www.ingramcontent.com/pod-product-compliance
Lightning Source LLC
Chambersburg PA
CBHW071714210326
41597CB00017B/2473